To Myrna —
With Thanks for your
Grace & light

A Deed to the Light

Love —

A Deed to the Light

Poems by Jeanne Murray Walker

University of Illinois Press
Urbana and Chicago

∞This book is printed on acid-free paper.

Library of Congress Cataloging-in-Publication Data
Walker, Jeanne Murray.
A deed to the light : poems / by Jeanne Murray Walker.
p.   cm.
ISBN 0-252-02922-4 (cloth : acid-free paper)
ISBN 0-252-07177-8 (pbk. : acid-free paper)
I. Title.
PS3573.A425336D44   2004
811'.54—dc22   2003021630

Acknowledgments

For permission to reprint earlier versions of some of these poems, I gratefully acknowledge the following periodicals:

The Christian Century: "Miss Leona Gifford's Hair," "Van Gogh," and "Wee Hours"
Cortland Review: "Outlaw"
Cresset: "Night-light" and "Sacrifice"
The Gettysburg Review: "Beyond Reading," "The Dutiful," and "Trying to Read *The Encyclopedia of Things No One Knows*"
Image: "After Terrorism," "Chaplin," and "Letter to a Friend Who Has Asked to Come"
The Journal: "How Mother Courage Saves Desdemona," "Insomnia," and "Luci's Knee"
Mars Hill Review: "Geese, Tree, Apple, Leaves"
The Nation: "Grasshopper"
The Notre Dame Review: "The Scarf"
Poetry: "After the Tornado," "Holding Back the Sun," "Light," and "Song of the Girl Who Stepped Out of Language"
Prairie Schooner: "Hunter"
Shenandoah: "Dinner Party," "Dung Beetle," "The Janitor," "Sewing," and "Stripping an Artichoke"
The Southern Review: "Letting Go" and "Melting Pot"
Spirituality and Health: "Making the Move"
Verse Daily: "Melting Pot"
West Branch: "Genius," "Mary Ellen Is Pregnant!" and "Myth"
Wheaton: "Portrait of the Virgin Who Said No to Gabriel"

Thanks also to the University of Delaware for a General University Research Fellowship, to the Pennsylvania Council on the Arts for a Fellowship, and to the Pew Foundation for a Fellowship in the Arts, all of which helped at every stage of this book's writing. I am grateful to E. Daniel Larkin, Elaine Terranova, Fleda Brown, and Deborah Burnham for their comments on the work and for their company along the way.

When a lovely flame dies, smoke gets in your eyes.

—Otto Harback

Now faith is the substance of things hoped for, the evidence of things not seen.

—Hebrews 11:1

Contents

Part 5

Part 6

Part 1

This Is to Say Good-bye: For Michiyo Ishii

Your bedroom. Your lover behind the bamboo screen.
He moves his flashlight across your tiny, silent woman's body
the way a searchlight sweeps dark sky,
the way, balancing in a boat one night,
on the muscley waters of the Amazon,
I ran a flashlight along the shore
until I spotted twin eye-fires
and felt the brain between them
pull me toward it. I aimed carefully and shot.

Today a friend called to say that you've been dead
for months, Japanese earth filling your eyes and mouth,
that your lover had a jealous wife,
that fearing we would discover him
and leak word back to his wife, you never told us,
and so many days you lay in your room alone,
like a seed inside its husk, being eaten by the cancer.
You were beautiful in your shyness.
You would laugh, holding your hand
over your crooked teeth. He hoarded
your beauty and we never got to say good-bye.
I would like to kill him, who imprisoned you
between your shyness and his need—
kill him and everything that kept me from you.
But surely it's not that simple. Nothing's
simple. I hope he held your hand the morning
you arose and walked out of your body

as easily, perhaps, as red ash flies up
from fire, moving swiftly, climbing
the stair steps of the sky, leaving the coal husk
of your smile like an afterthought
to us—to him, standing in the boat
of your bedroom, rocking a little
in his grief, crying, holding the gun on me—
and to me here in the hot Amazon
of anger, trying to forgive him.

Letter to a Friend Who Has Asked to Come

Till the roadwork on Route 70 loaned me words,
 I didn't know how to tell you. No. My
  shoulder's closed. No more trips here, Sister,

to weep over your lost babies. It gets
 harder to hear you over their jagged cries.
  Lightning cracking the sky in half at midnight.

Raw wakefulness. Them breathing
 next to me in bed. Why can't he hear them,
  your latest man, warming your hands

in your midtown restaurants? Maybe
 if you tried to climb the ladder of your grief
  at losing him, you could also lose

the habit of calling his house,
 his wife lifting the receiver as you whisper
  hello, hello. Or isn't the pressure of grief

enough to blow the lid off habit? Listen,
 I'm her! A wife. Have you noticed?
  When you called to tell me how you two danced,

you caught me with both hands in the diaper pail.
 Then hearing you, I would spin myself
  into your dark clubs, that sexy pivoting. I admit,

I loved slipping into your silk life! Oh, Sister,
 Sister, I have gone places in your body
  and been spared the doctor afterward!

And where are your children? You've seen mine.
 They're beautiful. They say they love me.
  The names of your children, scrawled

by lightning across this black night sky, are Emptiness
and Hunger. My God, emptiness and hunger!
And you, at the window, lonely.

Come. Come any time. The shoulder is always open.

Enough

Years later my mind was still going back
to the street where it happened,
dropping quarters into the parking meter
to keep the grudge going. Her crime was gossip,

was sharpening shafts of gossip,
piercing me till I bled like St. Sebastian.
I stood patiently where she put me,
only I wasn't patient.

Inside me rain poured—a thunderstorm,
wind wild enough to tear a roof off,
but inside, so she couldn't know what
she did wrong. After a few months

I couldn't remember either,
only that I had to keep tending
the grudge. Years later I still trekked back
to pay, exhausted, commuting

from some foreign city, the grudge,
my avocation. And then it ended.
One day it was gone. Like arriving
at work without recalling any drive

or any sights along the way.
Call it forgiveness. There must be
a hundred ways to forgive. But what I want
to say is how happy it made me,

how surprised. Like learning
the trip through Kansas will be shorter
than you thought, like learning death
is a window you can look out of.

Discovery

Yes, it may be true, suffering
    brings knowledge,
but last week I watched my friend

as he saw the honor he thought he'd earned
    bestowed upon his colleague,
and his eyes went blank as a hooked trout's

as he saw himself shrinking to a footnote
    in his friend's biography. He paced his cell,
dividing it in half, that half in half again,

his future shrinking more the more he paced it.
    I have seen the desperation
at fifty, what no one talks about,

when men have run out their strings,
    when they are as good
as they will ever be,

their houses on fire,
    their hopes burning like oil rags.
It is a luxury, his kind of pain,

what most people can't even dream of,
    his wife and children safe, plenty to eat,
but still, it's pain. The man who won

grew generous, sounded wisdom like the ocean,
    treated us to champagne, grew
taller. My friend stood smiling,

unbelieving, waiting to feel
    like a man who has lost a leg, balancing
in a landscape with no clear horizon.

The Nurses

I can hear them in there, laughing,
the nurses on the children's cancer ward,
as I walk through, my heart snagged
on a child in room 206, the boat of my hopes
tipping its freight into the water,
because kids in here are dying,
like trees turning in the fall
so slowly that we have to dwell
on each interval of suffering.

The door opens a slice and I see nurses
leaning into laughter, collapsing,
gripping each other's arms. Their laughter
skates on air, it fills the room up,
it towers above us. I shut the door.

They laugh because grief adheres to them
as desire adheres to beautiful women.
They have to pick it from their fur. They
have to help each other comb it out.
They study jokes as farm girls study
dresses in a catalog. They balance
on a high beam of laughter, knowing
if they laugh they might come back tomorrow.

—*For Jean Fergusson*

Hunter

I was reading in my office and
there she stood, my student,
metal shooting through her lip
and eyebrow like voltage,
her bruise-colored pants and T-shirt
tight as a doctor's glove,

finally talking, who never talked
in class. *I love the poems.* She said
these words shyly. *But you hate them,
don't you? You round them up
and torture them to make them confess.
You kill them!*

Eyes darting, she argued for
each reader making her own meaning.
She called it freedom.

I admit, I'd thought our class was going well,
thought of my students in their rooms
pursuing poems like happy beagles,
or sometimes settling together
with the wild tranquility
of swans onto a pond.

I thanked her for coming,
I said—perhaps with too much
confidence—that I'm for working it out
together. I'm for a language
we have to share.

She gazed at me, lost,
a fawn who'd strayed into a slaughterhouse.
She pulled a sleeve across her eyes
and said, *The book is an open field.*
Deer may graze all day,
but when hunters come,
the deer have to go home.

Oh, my child!

Lion

I hated the way you had to lift
your right arm to the podium with your left,
would have to lift it that way forever,
you who were once so dapper,
courtly, who played tennis

and hauled my box of books,
heavy as the ocean, to the fourth floor,
who lugged so many of us young poets
rung by rung down the fire escape
from stormy zeal to skill.

Before the sickness found you,
we walked my campus,
you, wise as usual, guessing how
beneath those squares of violent green grass
there must be heat pipes,

and after that I could imagine
a universe below
of ducts and tubes and carillons
and pipes with constellations
of furnaces, wine storage,

a long passage, maybe, leading
to a chamber orchestra, and why not
in hot weather, an aqua pool
where the violinists take a dip between
the slow movement and the vivace?

The day I heard about your death,
I remembered what you'd taught me,
I grasped the metal ring on the trapdoor,
pulled it easily as a pop-top,
and climbed down stairs

to the place you'd shown me,
to find you sitting
under a blue umbrella, revising.
I saw you squinting, rising,
smiling, coming toward me,

holding out your two good arms.

Stripping an Artichoke

As we watch the moon drag in old night
on her cold-hearted hook,
we take turns stripping and eating
an artichoke. What a disastrous day!

Disastrous. Well, a day in June
with rudbeckia and gloriosa daisies
hip high outside the window,
the dying of our sick friends slowed down,
by radiation, apparently, to match the pace

of our own dying. To tell the truth,
it was a day of minor setbacks. And I admit,
it wasn't an artichoke we ate,
it was asparagus, elegant and easy,
a vegetable with no bad points.

I called it an artichoke just now, maybe,
because that brings up honesty,
because of how you have to work
to get to the core. Think of
the woman who first guessed
that that ugly prickpuss knot of green

might save her starving children.
How hungry did she have to be
to pick it, eat it raw, hoping
it wasn't poison, go to bed retching,
get up sleepless at 2 A.M., guessing it needed

to be cooked? Look. The moon
is shining. She's peeling the leaves off,
the way a person might strip away
lies and melodrama and self-pity.
She's beautiful and comic, her whole self
converging on that core. Keep your eyes
on her, raising her knife.

Dinner Party

We lounge amid the wreckage of this lovely evening,
next to little pelts of scooped-out cantaloupe
on blue Spanish plates, while Billie Holiday
drifts through us like fog through trees.
We have almost made it together inside loneliness,
almost reached that perfect shadowy place
where it doesn't matter what we say, the others
grasp it. We are chords in a new progression
into stillness, a new rendition of "All of Me,"
though none of us, if asked, could tell
what taught us such love was possible.

And then suddenly we're back in history,
as if a gust of gravity had swept in. Or
the rubber band snapped. And we're pulling on
our coats, reaching for polite good-bye phrases
like rain hats, remembering there's happiness
at home, too, and a Posturepedic mattress
and a dog to walk. We look plain again,
standing around like extras in a movie.
What happened among us may be true and secret.
It may be everything. But the night won't talk,
and none of us can find the word to loosen
its tongue. It was fun, we say later. It was fun.

—*For Greg and Lysa*

Part 2

Sacrifice

Sometimes I think of Bach,
working a stick with his mouth
to get notes he couldn't reach
with his hands and feet,

so the sweet catastrophe of counterpoint
could break the hearts of his parishioners.
And while we're on the subject of music,
think of the monk who dove

and dove again into dark archives
to rescue from oblivion
the Gregorian chants of Leonin and Perotin,
whose names have lasted while his remained unknown,

though what they've dubbed him,
Anonymous IV, makes him less unknown
than other unknown writers.
Still, in the sacrifice business,

there's no guarantee of fame.
Remember Annabel Lee Stein, whose brain
crawled backward (*drawkcab*)
through the little halls of words?

I bet no one can recall the teacher
who for years sat patiently coaxing
Annabel Lee to read. *Sacrifice*
is slow as a funeral procession

in rush-hour traffic, the sort of word
other words pass, honking
And still, God (*doG*) is not
the only one who sacrificed,

as Annabel Lee could tell you,
Annabel, a grandmother now,
standing by the stove, moving her lips
as she reads a cake-mix box.

Chaplin

Maybe suffering is always like this,
as black and white and silent
as the little man pacing his jail cell,
his suit suddenly grown too tight,
his hands gripping the cold bars
while he cranes his neck to see
whether his beautiful woman still waits
for him at the table set in their shack.

There is no jailer, that's how it is.
Or else the jailer gives him a look
as if to say, *You put yourself in here,*
Buster, now find your own way out.
This funny crumbsuck of a man, no
Robert Redford, I can tell you,
more like a heart on legs.

When we see a close-up of the girl,
her pointy lips and white catastrophic face,
we guess that she won't spring him,

and even with all our longing, we can't,
we, who are prisoners in our own lives,
their iron gates unlocking only rarely—
for instance, the way some technician
learned to transfer old film to this video
so we can watch the little man's heart break,

the way my friend's did, for example,
slowing her dead lover's last message
on the answering machine, dwelling on each
grainy vowel until her possibilities
seemed as small as Chaplin's in his cell.

And then what sometimes happens,
happens. Something changes
its mind, the door swings open,
as if brushed by God's finger
as he chanced to amble by,
and the dazed man walks free.
We see a long shot of him toddling
toward the girl, still at the table,
waiting, his bowlegs scissoring
the air, his feet turned out,
his jaunty black head bobbing. You might say
sound and color have kicked in.
You can almost hear petals falling
from the apple tree he passes, white petals
drifting across the brilliant, purple sky.

Genius

Flying fingers, the final chord,
and young Mozart, dazed,
squints beyond the footlights as
the rhythm of applause
urges his muscles to more music
and he looks down at his matching set of hands,
separated at birth,
which call to one another
like lonely birds
across continents of muscle and bone.

Now his blood swoops and caws
so he has to bow and walk off
to find a paper to write on,
but the conductor leads him back
where stage lights pin him down
so the audience can see him:
jerking, pirouetting before them.

This monstrous gift! he thinks,
I'm nothing but the earth
trembling when god dances.
Love is what he wants, and quiet.
But his fingers curve to cage the second movement of
his next opus, springing into his mind so madly—
when a woman in her blue gown
hops onto the stage like
a cadenza
in his—already!—unfolding third movement
and what if
he can't remember it
to write it down—and now

he feels her cool hair against his cheek!
So it's possible, he thinks. A woman.
He prays to find the doorknob,
walk out of the music,
kiss her
from some part of himself that means it,
be granted, just, oh God, one day
with her in silence.

Van Gogh

All right, I love him for the way
    he painted *Vermilion! Orange!* jagged as
  shouts, and when no one bought them,
    no one even heard him,
he shouted louder,
    Sunflowers! Self-portrait!
and years later, not one sold,
    he cut off his own ear.

Then he had to bring it back on canvas
    hundreds of times,
  in the brass swelling
  of the bell
that called him to dinner,
  in the complicated iris
    at the end of the asylum path.
      Think how stooping
at a fork in the road
    he might have seen a stone-shaped ear,
how the human heart,
    once it knows what it needs,
will find it everywhere, how
    in the curve of his delicately padded cell
      one starry night, he must have murmured
      everything he had ever wanted to say
straight into the ear of God.

Uncle Lloyd: His Eight Types of Courage

This is the house his parents left him,
the shy boy who never learned to ride,
here's the snarling furnace he feared at night,
the sigh of water rising on its elbows
in the drain to find him.

These are the Minnesota clouds he asked
to rain on his corn.

And here's the iron bed in the basement
where he lay, looking up
to see, maybe, a slice of navy sky
where clouds rushed west like splendid horses.

The living room, 40 degrees,
where he sat in his coat and earflaps,
unwrapping our Christmas presents.

The cold-water tap he turned on,
standing on one foot, then
the other under the icy spray,
scrubbing his calloused knees with Comet.

This is how he shaved, drawing
the dry blade across his face. No mirror.

And the large-print Bible he tried to read
that day, letters forking like lightning
in his brain, as he looked into the wedge of sky.
Here are the three suits he laid out, leaving
the choice to us, to the undertaker, who cared?
Because he'd guessed a way to ride,
catching a saddle, swinging onto
the back of the final horses galloping west.

Sniper

Somewhere a woman is beginning to suspect her husband.
Oh, the warning signs, she knows—his rants, political hatreds,
but she loves the way his dark eyes taper, his nostrils flare.
After sex with him she sleeps in the crook of his arm.
She laughs with his sister. She helped bury his mother.

I am here, trying to hate him. Standing by the swollen river,
I study the place he jumped. He hides under the water.
He can't hear the dogs, baying their manhunt into
the pine trees. I want to call to him. *Swim!*
Get away! When I return to my life, beside you,

they are bearing out his last victim, and the TV
says *mystery,* says he's got no pattern, unlike
the Zodiac killer, who scribbled a big dipper of death
across our city. The sniper ventures into malls now,
like an addict on heroin. They say he needs

a bigger hit each time. To hunt him, they tell us,
they've rented infrared detectors. America wants him
dead. We tend bonfires of hatred. We are lit from
the inside with hatred. Hatred binds us together. I close
my eyes and try to hold him steady enough to hate him,

but it's her face I see, readable as my sister's.
She's opening a can of soup. I step into her kitchen,
past his gun, leaning against the wall. I can't stop myself
from taking her face in my hands. She would
love anything. She will never forget the good in him.

How Mother Courage Saves Desdemona

Desdemona is sobbing in the bedroom, a hole
in her heart, when Mother Courage strides in
wearing black-tie shoes, to switch on the lamp.

She has just driven her wagon
across Europe to find her dead daughter, Katrin,
stripped the body to sell her shirt,

and then walked aimlessly all night.
At the door she hears a young woman sobbing.
She whispers tenderly, *Here, Little Sausage, blow*

on your hem. She wants to pull Desdemona from
her extravagant belief in her own downfall.
Because what is a handkerchief, the old woman asks,

but a certain way of thinking about the world,
a flutter in the wind, anybody's wind.
If you aren't careful, you nest in one man's pocket

and then whoosh, you turn up in another's.
But you are a precious clue, the only real thing
in the play! You can't trust a man

whose name begins with O! When he mutters,
Turn out the light, *Sheepface, Daughter, Desdemona,*
YOU are the light! Given what that Moor did,

you should be ashamed to leave a trail of boo-hoos
like snail tracks across Europe!
Get up! It's time to find another play.

Mother Courage goes on scrubbing past romance,
down to the very floorboards of love. Together they rise.
Now they are walking past us down the aisle,

holding hope in their hands as if it were
a cup of tea. They exit this script to find another,
striding out of the fiction, into their own lives.

—*For Susan Sweeney*

Portrait of the Virgin Who Said No to Gabriel

This is the one Giotto never painted.

She looked up from baking that morning, hearing
his feathers settle and his voice scatter like gold coins
on the floor. He told her, his forehead sweaty
from the long trip. *Me?* she breathed, *Oh sure!*

But after he walked away, she couldn't forget his look,
the strange way his feet rang like horseshoes on the stones.
What she'd been wanting before he interrupted
was not the Bach *Magnificat,* I can tell you, not stained
glass. Nothing risky. Just to keep her good name.

Small as she was, how could she keep in her heart
those centuries of praise? But I praise her
anyway for wanting a decent wedding
with napkins folded like hats and a good Italian wine.
I praise her name, Lenora. I praise the way

she would practice carefully, making the *L*
like a little porch, where she could imagine standing
to throw a red ball to some children she loved.
I praise the way, year by year, she let herself see
who that visitor was. Think of her collecting

belief slowly, the way a bird builds her nest
in an olive tree. Then finally how one year,
after the leaves fell, she was an old woman
looking at the truth, outlined against
the salmon sky, knowing it was true.

For not despising her own caution then, I praise her.
For never feeling envy. And for the way, once,
she stepped past her fear to hand a cup of water
to a thirsty carpenter fainting by her door.

In every room of this gallery I think I see her picture.

—*For Henry William Griffin*

Part 3

Birthday

It was years before I grasped how, if I wrote it,
no one would believe me, how the phone rang
as I was getting dressed, as I was listening
to my mother sing in the kitchen on her birthday,

happy, finally, after two years as a widow—
missing him in a different way, maybe, humming
about the miracle of reaching one more station,
even without him, the power of her body

to keep her children in clothes, in food, the miracle
that she has strength to walk to work and back,
that someone pays her for what she loves to do,
that God gives us no more grief than we can bear

and now her oldest child—imagine!—at college
where she wanted to be once herself, poised on the lip
of knowledge, and so her September morning
opened like a door into the sky, into some greater

likelihood, and when the phone rang
it might have been her good stars calling to ask
whether they had the right address, it might
have been joy with a marriage proposal—

all of which came later—but this was a voice
that told her my brother was dead, how he was
sorry, how her son was with Jesus now, how
no one knew what happened, and I slunk in

and watched as if I were our dog, Rags; I learned
entirely from the way her shoulders slumped,
and her voice weakened like worn cloth, I knew,
I knew, since I had been schooled in the ways

of grief, and yet when she straightened herself
to tell me, she was a mountain, she was huge
and shining, on her forehead I saw hope,
and you will not believe me, it was enough.

Miss Leona Gifford's Hair

Long before my father died
we whispered how Miss Gifford was bald.
That's why she wore her wimple
summer and winter, to hide her loss,
we said. And I thought, the way I tried to
hide mine. Because after we buried my tall father,
he still cast a shadow, heaped up in his death,
filling the four corners of the world,
and whatever light the teachers tried to throw
against my mind's wall—
the good and holy beacons of history and science—
were blocked by the shadow of my father.
When my friends felt its cold edges creep toward them
they wouldn't touch me, they scattered
like magnets fleeing from another magnet.
I sat alone at recess on the slatted bench.
One day Miss Gifford held out her thimble hand to me.
I heard her say, *Help me carry these books.*
With my shadow hands I picked up her books
and walked beside her to her office,
where she lifted their mortal weight from me.

Oh sing, Muse, of how she turned
and stripped off the black cape that we said
made her fly like Zorro,
how she unlaced the black rowboats that we said
made her skim across the River Styx,
how she took off the wire-rims
that made her eyes small as a pig's,
how the blue eyes were wet,
how she said, *I'm sorry, child,*
how she looked small and thin and trembled like a wet cat
when she untied her scarf
and shook out her blonde hair like a gift
into the darkness.

Making the Move

We are sitting on the floor, sorting
your rock collection, sending the granite
back to the earth, the mica schist to the box
marked SAVE. I love the geode.

Jack, I say, and mention its shine.
You hold it in your palm, deciding.
Outside, it's raining, proof that no sooner
do you get to know the sky than it moves on.

Tomorrow the moving van arrives.
Your father and I have signed the paper.
This is the last day I will touch the door
where I turned so many times to feed you

and met myself, turning. But your voice is
changing. You throw me a glance: *This nostalgia's
prehistoric.* You turn the geode over. What if
we are nothing, I wonder, but the stones we choose

to keep? *Jack!* I say, this time for
everything we dare not throw away.
You have tossed *The Odyssey* aside.
I think of the man who never stopped moving

and called it twenty years of life,
remembering the chapter where he talks
to his heart, how he says, *Old Friend,*
you who have gone everywhere with me,

when the testing comes, do not burst.
He knew how little he could carry
in his knapsack and still call it Home.
He would have kept this, I think,

the split geode, gleaming like a hundred amethysts.
As you toss it in the garbage
I don't even move to save it,
the old stalwart rock, my heart, my heart.

To My Son, Off to College

We stand there in our vestibule, me clutching
my car keys, you, your suitcase,
me about to recite the names of apples,

winesap, braeburn, etc., the way poets
recite them, then to chant the names
of poets, too, anything you'll listen to,

stanzas of lightning from red mouths.
It isn't loveliness I'm after, I can tell you,
it's any damn thing that keeps your hand

from pushing that door open. Though you're
long gone already. And I know it's wrong,
when the heart has stopped, to pretend it hasn't.

Like a taxidermist. No, we're mixed up
with time, my Love, and poetry, as usual,
fails to stop you. You have to go away,

and you may not be back.
I eat one of the apples in your memory,
like a pioneer who's down to eating seed corn,

the sweet-sour juices running into a future
without you, while a voice tells me
I don't own you, you were a gift, and

my barbaric unteachable mother heart doesn't get it,
thinks, Okay, fine, so you're gone now,
you're that much closer to coming back.

Letting Go

I walk through abandoned fields of our house,
the chairs shrinking from me like wounded
horses. The rug crying out under my feet.
From cupboards comes the sound of cracking dishes,
accusing. I was wrong to leave you at the airport.
The house wants you. I climb to your room
and kneel, trying to breathe you in,
but you're not here.
In a different room, inside my head,
I see my grandmother, her gray hair hanging
to her waist. *Let it go,* she tells me
as she washes her feet in a dimpled tin pan.
She butchered lambs, then asked their pardon on her knees
by the blazing wood stove where she cooked them.
My grandmother wipes her terrible feet.
She is old enough. She has learned how to trust.
I think of God, how he lets the universe go,
the oceans breaking down the land,
stars wheeling toward the dangerous rim.
I wonder if he trusts it, the whole
savage, delicately rigged-up thing.

The Dogs of the Heart

Two weeks without you now, and look,
no hands, my heart rides without falling
until I come across this stranger here in London,
her face oddly like your face,
a field shifting under windblown rain,
and I realize how your mouth
can make your face do lovely things
and I am lost, thinking how one thing becomes

another, how in Pipestone National Park
I once saw a rock dissolve into
the face of a lost Indian chief
I thought might call out to me.

What is that chief, what is this woman,
what's any of it but reminders of your absence?
Of absence, period. Of how your absence
can slip its leash and bay like a hound.

And who can quiet them once they start,
these dogs of the heart, Absence, Desire, Longing?
I am rummaging in the grab bag of London,
thinking that any city can turn bad-tempered
and let out dogs like these,
their noses tough as black rubber to track us down,
their instinct to bite and never to let go.

Rain

Now, with you asleep beside me,
with the small kingdom of our yard
bewildered by months of sun,
water table sinking, signs on I-95 urging

SAVE WATER—nevertheless I wake up
cursing this rainy morning,
dead ringer for the Sunday
medics removed my father's body

from our house, when Art and Marilyn Johnson
drove me through the downpour
in the back seat of their Chevy
so no one would have to pry him

from my hands, because he had already
drifted away, spilled over the waterfall
where I couldn't follow, like a noble warrior
launched into his new life, his skiff

receding on the river, like a fisherman
competent finally in the mystery
of the oldest fish's mind,
flowing, passing beyond me.

I get out of the Johnson's car, having spent
too many years in it already,
and thank them for their effort,
and begin to reason with myself.

Love this rain, I say. I say we need it.
I hear chipping sparrows welcoming.
Whatever comes, whatever comes.
You smile in your sleep and turn over.

Even now you are moving in a country where
I cannot go. Outside, creatures are floating away.
The liquid cry of a cat.
Rivers, passing by our window.

Night-light

Through the window cruel stars
glitter. Snails must be freezing
in their tiny hideouts. Not even Bach
has the heart to go on. I flick the light
on, the small one, so the room won't
jump into its lurid daytime clothes.
You turn over and sigh. When we
collided last night, basalt heaved up
from some Pleistocene age. We reared
against one another, huge, obstructionist,
our voices molten lava, our language
on fire. But God has a sense of
humor. Even murderers must sleep
at last, and we were mown down
by the sandman. Now you lie here,
your normal size again and furry.
Our wooden sandpiper cocks its one foot
safely on our dresser. The night-
light fits everything back into its own
skin. I lay my hand on your sleeping
arm, suddenly able to imagine
myself: *after you.* Then you,
no, after you.

Part 4

Light

And then there was Mr. Luman, the teacher
whose death they announced that Tuesday,
who vowed to donate ten thousand dollars

to the one of us who named our first kid
Igor Stravinsky—just send him a telegram
to let him know, he said. He'd cut off

his thumbs for culture. He'd be happy
to dive five stories naked from the window
to make us understand "To be or not to be."

He knew we thought he had no real life,
that he was a cardboard cutout
they wheeled from the closet

every morning. And really, what was he
but the longing to instill in us
The Finer Things? He was nothing

but echoes that lingered after the last note
of Beethoven's Fifth. He dodged through
subjects like a bumper car. He had to teach us

everything! He begged the boys not
to wear hats in class, to see *The Nutcracker.*
That final day when the bell rang he was

still talking about Queen Elizabeth, how
Lord Burleigh brought a ten pound note
to the coronation to buy back the British crown

from God, who is the true king. I unfolded
my bright limbs and filed past him to math.
The last thing I heard him say before he met the train

at the blind crossing was how he loved Hamlet,
how he wanted to be Hamlet, the one character
who knew enough to write the play he's in.

Outlaw

May he go among the imperishable stars,
May he journey in the boat of a million years.
—The Book of Going Forth by Daylight

You've taken off again, J.R., this time
steering the boat of your coffin
into the final terror you always wooed,
leaving me to read your obit

and make plans with February,
its snow already gone filthy under the cedar,
which I now declare your shrine.

You were no good, our neighbors said,
needing an indigenous criminal. Well,
you did have a mouth to make Marilyn Monroe
blush, with which you kissed me under the old cedar.
You, who taught me to laugh at death
while you gunned the 1952 Chevy. The only one
who would still touch me after my father died.
Who taught me rage is better than fear.

But it wasn't love, was it,
that night you held me in the front seat,
the night you wouldn't let me go,
while I imagined my mother, frantic as scalding soup,
phoning neighbors, sweating—my widowed mother—?

Then what made you hold me
till I could see the ghost of my father
like a bearded cedar walking through the dark?

The Janitor

Muse, I'll put down my fiddle
while you sing it *a capella*
the song of barrel-chested Roy,
Roy of the suspenders, Roy
redolent of sweeping compound,
Roy who studied the blue hardcover
Meditation Exercises of Loyola
on the toilet in the boy's room,
Roy who'd lost his arm in WWII,
who kept a ferret he called Lefty
in a bamboo cage. Baptist Roy,
Roy, the part-time minister the jail called
since no one else would go
to pray with the murderer
before they put him in the chair
for stabbing seven nurses.
Roy the next day telling how
the man's face glistened, saying
that he was awfully, truly sorry.
Sing Sweet Girl, Sweet Muse,
of Roy's stump squirming in the air,
of how his name was our curse,
how anyone we disdained was a *Roy*.
Sing how he cleaned our windows,
straightened our galoshes,
patched our books. How he polished
every sink until it shone like heaven.

Song of the Girl Who Stepped Out of Language

What could I say? *I have fallen*
in love? If I had known
language for it, would that have changed things?
He'd have gone on shuffling
Latin flash cards with those articulate hands—
Veni, vidi, vici—

while we waited for the bus
at the dusk end of day,
beyond Latin Club. I grew silent
as a granite wall.
             Periwinkle flashed
at my feet like fallen stars, a waterfall
of ivy cascaded over me, and
children walked by, serenading
the sky like Canada geese flying south.

There is an opening between day
and night, an aperture in the evening shadows
where everything happens. But till then,
I didn't know there is no word for it.

Mary Ellen Is Pregnant!

Like watching that red truck squeal
around the corner in a cloud of dust
and turn over, spilling thousands
of tea bags onto the road, like watching
firemen hose it down till tea flows
down gutters, over sidewalks, like seeing
grandmothers stream from houses,
scooping cups of it, the whole neighborhood
gathering together on curbs for tea,
drinking the truck disaster. That's what it's like,
finding out that Mary Ellen is pregnant.
The news is real as rock. It is a diamond.
I pass it to my friends and they pass it to theirs.
Each of us touches it, rubs it, shines it
till it glints. Bored, thirsty for catastrophe,
we can't get enough. Between classes
we want to walk beside her, we want to carry
her books, we want her to signal us
when the child moves inside her.
She smiles, the queen of secrets
who has slipped into a foreign land
without a passport, the girl who has
swallowed the sun and will give off
only what light she wants to.

Holding Back the Sun

I step on the gas, my stomach riding
the small knoll that counts as a hill
outside Lincoln, Nebraska, thrilled at the boy,
his red and black letter jacket, all mine,
the capable arms, the beautiful nape,
the mouth talking baseball beside me
in the crash seat. As we approach
ninety, I shift, a glissando into
another key. "Love Me Tender, Love
Me True" on the radio. Elvis found
words for what I can't mention.
Maybe he could say why in our bodies
I feel such heat rising, the whole sun
bursting through a small aperture
in the earth. We might as well be
running separate and wordless
down the slopes of a shaking volcano.
Where will we end up? We don't mention
this either. Maybe that's why,
at night in bed alone, I have to touch
my breasts and try to predict whether
nature will erupt next Friday or later,
whether anyone can hold back the sun,
and how a person can live afterward.
I press my foot, the needle shimmies
toward a hundred, while both of us pretend
that nothing's up. In my mind I hear
my mother say to no one in particular,
Where did I go wrong? She's standing
by our kitchen window, staring at the backyard
where my sister is imagining a barn for the horse
she longs to buy. We are all knee deep
in fantasy. Mother peels potatoes
at the center of the universe, scheming
how to pay the mortgage, her mind rubbing
accidentally over me, alert to the danger

that I will, eventually, be blasted from her.
What I want to know is how I can remember
this gearshift, this boy, this speed
which never happened? How fast I must have lived,
home at my desk, coveting the ends of
the known world, reading, reading, reading.

Sewing

I remember, that morning, how
I stayed home from school to sew a dress,
how I began by watching snow
drape the city. Pour it out, Muse,
how I tended the window, how I was
patience itself, how still
I sat, how I became
the chair. And that's when
you flocked down, drowsy angel,
clever seamstress. Say anything,
say how those mothy flakes
charmed you, how you tucked
the snow around the buildings,
how you swathed them,
how you worked with the material,
how you were nowhere visible
but in the spaces.
          Sing how, that afternoon,
when I laid out the flimsy pattern
dancing around the fabric on my knees
the rug's whiskers buffing them
till they were numb and rosy,
I squinted at the arrow on the bias,
dovetailed the plackets,
made Tab 1A kiss Tab 1B.
As I pointed the sharp snout of scissors
and whispered, *Dear Lord, make me*
good at geometry, don't let me
ruin this,
     as I started to cut,
I could feel myself move
beyond the pattern, move
toward beauty, move toward
the empty spaces.

Part 5

After Terrorism

Here is the path, I'd like to say, darker than it was, maybe,
but here we are. Turn left at the light. What light is left.

I am thinking about Romulus Augustus, the two-year-old, last
emperor of Rome, how one morning before Barbarians
broke through the wall and slashed his throat, his guardian
stood on his portico looking out and said, *So that was Rome,*

which had been falling for a hundred years
slowly as an encroaching stain through fabric,
as the invasion of ginko forests across Eastern Europe,

though no one had noticed. Maybe the John Deere of history
has to drag catastrophe into our library with an 18-gauge chain
before we finally stand up and say, *Well, what have we got here?*
It is the divide I'm talking about, the crack you finally notice
in the champagne glass, though truthfully, what strikes you first
is that you won't be finishing the champagne you love.

We are divided. The towers have fallen, and terrorists
may be secreted like candied fruit through the whole loaf—
at the skating rink, at the post office,
in Super Cuts, a chartreuse-haired barber wielding his scissors.

I want us to get out of this together, the way a family
might cross a meadow under storm-laden clouds,
the skinny girl cartwheeling, the father pushing his mother's
wheelchair, the young married couple holding hands.

Listen. Outside this frame I can see light,
heavy as pardon, reliable as granite.
Help me. Help me drag it into the picture.

—*For my students*

Melting Pot

As the alarm shrilled through the twelve-seater,
    as the pilot scrambled for his manual,
        I wanted someone to stand up
and lead us in song,
    or possibly a prayer

but we sat beneath our personal
    air nozzles, unable to shake
        our useful habit of reserve.
Beside me a man read *Newsweek.*
    A girl pulled out her barf bag

and I thought of sending my voice out
    like a skater on a pond to say something
        true and beautiful and daring,
how not a sparrow, maybe,
    falls without notice,

but our plane was yo-yoing
    like a heart machine gone bonkers
        graphing the steep *W*'s
of our collective fall
    and my voice burrowed

for safety in my chest
    as I turned, we all turned
        to our captain, a simple boy in earphones
fighting to steer the little duck
    paddling for its life

in a dark, anonymous sky
    and I thought how odd it was
        that our names would appear
together in the papers,
    like the cast of a musical,

we who each died alone, without ritual or touching.

Wee Hours

How innocent we where back then . . . last Monday.
—Roger Angell

You wake, uneasy, to the fleet wind rattling
your door, your mind scrambling for

what? Not this slip and blab of raindrops,
not the bell tolling. The towers again?

A sniper? This time a child, maybe, at the trigger.
With a shudder your old life turns sideways

and slips behind the wind, throwing
the moon off balance. You're practicing pain,

rousing the lion of terror so when
it turns the corner and eats your heart

you won't be caught off guard. When
it will find you can't be counted on.

Only a few things can be counted on. The sun.
The old sun rising. The grass growing.

The same sky doling out the same blue
and children shaking out their petals

in the school yard every day, even that day.

Control

It was, maybe, three that morning, light rain,
me driving 70 m.p.h. back from New York,
touching the hand of the woman in the tollbooth

who didn't wear gloves, who offered her palm
like a big hollyhock, open to chances
as I was open when my Toyota found the oil slick

under the high lurid lamps, oil flashing
the broken blues and pinks of a rainbow trout,
and the car veered, suave as a dancer, into oncoming traffic.

Turn into the skid, they tell you, but it takes balls
to turn toward a sixteen-wheeler at point-blank range
and then the spin came, the long slow twisting

as in a movie, the road rotating sideways
up the windshield, light poles skidding, trees
standing on their heads, sky torn out by its roots,

oh, then time stretched out, it lengthened,
not monstrously, but sweetly as the taffy
we pulled in Lincoln, Nebraska, long ropes of it,

as if there could not be enough catastrophe
to fill up the time. Each part stretched out luxuriously
as if I would live forever and this crash would be,

henceforth, my life. Then I heard the rasp
of tearing metal, the car sailing to its final
destination, the crash, far away and righteous

in the silent night, an echo in the cornfields.
I will tell you, just before my head struck
the wheel, I glimpsed again for a second

what I have to overlook, perhaps, to live—
that I did not create the world, that if I live,
I live through someone else's kind permission.

Writing the Novel

On the day the story comes to me, the chapters
hang like cured hams from twine. Easy, I think.
All I have to do is push aside the dark
to cut them, stuff them into my burlap bag.
That's how this winter will go by, I think,
all day sitting at my desk in jeans and old socks,
pushing the salty flesh through the little language
peephole so the story comes out like the alphabet
lined up in rows. And then at dusk
to drink a glass of cabernet, talk to my husband,
careful not to say anything about the story.
Because I know nothing I can tell him about the story,

for instance, I cannot tell him how this afternoon
it came for me like a living thing, rude, not
well spoken, but shambly, its bones clattering like the oak
as it stepped from its dark hole in our yard, and I felt earth
bucking, saw the willow tossing her hair
like a woman on her hands and knees, trying
to get away. What I know connected to what
I don't know, all of it climbing through my window,
crouching in the corner of my office, its snouty breath,
the rattle in its throat, its black lips and yellow fangs.
The alphabet fell away like a foolish dream. Quick and
rampant, the story leapt onto my desk where it can grow.

The Dutiful

You pity them, yes. But they know how
to make you need them. I'm thinking
of my grandmother with her dutiful dinners

as I grope in the dark downstairs
to fix the circuit breaker—another duty
of the dutiful. If the dutiful are too preoccupied

for moonlight, you can't blame the moon,
who climbs out of bed, and, noticing they're missing,
shines anyway. Think of them in the morning,

writing lists: *take laundry, pick up milk.*
They barely taste their toast and eggs. Their eggs,
you might say, float somewhere out of reach,

a vision escaping, like the breasts of Diana in the Uffizi,
which, if they ever saw it, would escape them, too.
Think of them composing lists right through

hundreds of breakfasts which are not breakfasts.
Think of their malnourishment, of their mad caution,
of how they shy away from too much hope.

Try to love them. It could be me, the shadow
you see turning the corner from the bus stop
later this afternoon, walking toward you,

its face pleasant, its mind climbing
rung by rung down lists.

Beyond Reading

That day the sun was dazzling, no hint
of what would happen, only the discovery
that we had already burned the trees, back shed,
attic floor, bookshelves. If we wanted to live,

we would have to burn books.
Reading was my religion. I would weep
at shutting the cover, returning
to the shallow, disappointing world.

That first day, to keep from freezing,
we chose between a high school text
and a political pamphlet. Why
did I rejoice in a new kind of freedom,

as if I were flying or just being born?
We whispered to one another of how things
can weigh a person down, of how lucky
we were that we had hoarded books

we didn't need. But each night
got harder. Pulp novels, instruction books
for appliances. Bad poetry,
then good poetry. The long cold days

when we had nothing to do
were filled up with ravenous debate
about what to burn that night.
I argued to save the ancient illuminated

manuscript, but they voted me down.
We would burn it last. Looking into its fire,
I saw how I had feared this, nothing more
to read. But it felt exquisite to be alive,

talking together, lovely to be
warming our hands at the same fire—
even one built from the thin paper
of the book I had loved the most.

Cleaning Out

I'm getting rid of it all this time, gadgets first,
the elegant little box of tools for decanting wine,
for instance. I am going mad with clutter,

all day driving for light bulbs, lawn fertilizer,
obeying my refrigerator. The cat is my boss.
Even the VCR tells me where to go,
meanwhile inside me, a whole army destitute
as the soldiers who wintered at Valley Forge,
barefoot, their ammunition gone.

I begin by hauling out the little toolbox
which a torturer might use to drill
through a child's eardrum.
Or just as easily it might be, say,
a jeweler's kit. I lay that possibility
on the junk pile with it.

I haul out my books, the wounded spines,
the long lines of letters—their arguments for being kept—
but I haul them out anyway.
I work for hours till shadows bunch up in the corners.
I am sweating, barbaric.
Crowding around me like beasts,
each piece of furniture makes a case for its existence.

No, I say, *get rid of it all.*
I am opening the French doors.
I am letting the sky in.

Let my walls stand like broken sentences
among the flashing spaces.

Dung Beetle

On that brief Alexandrian afternoon
when he carved a beetle,
light stayed a little longer
so he carved beetles
on insignias and rings and amulets,
and when luck rose modestly in the sky
he sent the beetles to other cities
and his friends wrote him
that his scarab on their mantle
made their marriage flourish,
that when they laid a beetle
on their son's blind eye, sight flashed up
like a rabbit from a hat

until finally everyone in Egypt believed
that the beetle who lays its eggs in dung
could make them immortal.

Who can tell what sustains us? Who can say
why God's heart beats in small things?
Under the skyscraper that raises its eyebrows
to keep counsel with clouds—
listen.
Deep in the earth, clear water runs.

Trying to Read *The Encyclopedia of Things No One Knows*

I'd like to pull it from the shelf
to learn the date they'll fill in too soon
to the right of the dash (1944–   )
and the names of people I will meet and love
before then, as well as planets they'll find
and the face of the baby
who will appear nine months after
my daughter gets pregnant.

But who can read it?
When I hold it up to the light,
I can see through it. It's more stealthy
than one hand clapping, a program
printed without toner. It's a breath
between a pair of sighs. And what I can
read there, I keep forgetting, its taillights
disappearing in the dark before me,

only without the headlights or the dark.
Some mercy must keep these pages blank.
Who would have courage to go on,
understanding her own future?
But if I could, I'd check it out anyway,
carry it home under my arm like a shadow
and read it late at night,
keeping myself small and helpless and interested.

Part 6

Boundaries

"Good fences make good neighbors."
—Robert Frost

It's a big country, live and let live, free to be
you and me, etc., with malls like monuments
to Freedom and also with the big, idiot prairie,
where you can choose which cow to talk to.

Oh Freedom's famous in America, but sometimes
I think of the fence Frost praised, or pretended to,
the way you can bisect a hillside and presto, two
hillsides, one for each of you. How you can

draw a line across a paper and have both earth
and sky. Think how a fence can be five thin wires,
like a bass clef that runs on for miles
guarding wheat and soybeans, the way

a campaign speech might drone on. And less
flimsy, I can tell you, than the barricade of air
between my study and the living room
where my son stands right now, threatening

to ask for clean socks. Where would we be
without boundaries, including fragile ones
like the line between land and water, where the ocean
lies down like a golden retriever in a downstay

so faithful that glaciers will melt before he alters
his obedient heart? Or without the horizon
that goes on mumbling its secret mantra
at the edge of wheat fields, no matter how many

developments we erect to blot it out?
And I'd like to praise the way we have invented
our own small boundaries, the basketball rim
where the nervous fat ball hangs out

to discover its fate: to score or, sadly, not.
And the edge of this page, where the world begins again.
And the actual bass clef—call it a five-wire fence—
that holds Bach's counterpoint, which,

in the next room, keeps trying to break out,
like my son, who has shattered the air lock now,
and walks into my study, all smiles, all charm.

Myth

I am thinking of those who never lost faith
when the brontosaurus unlatched from facts
and drifted up toward myth. Who still loved him
after learning that he was forged
from different skeletons. Who admire
the fat root of tail that keeps him from tipping over.
Who have grown fond of the tiny head
he holds up like a lantern to light him through the gallery.

Think of the tiny woman with the humpback
who comes at night and climbs the ladder
to dust the prehistoric skin, who in the morning,
after her momentous job, ties her plastic rain hat
under her chin and waits for the bus.

Think of the scientist, even,
combing the archives, glancing at the map
of the giant body, wearing combat boots
in case he needs to enter another bog
and root around for the odd femur or clavicle,
who felt his fame rise like a fever, who is
proud as a father of having made the whole thing up
from a few used bones.

                    Think of the boy skipping
out of the museum store, launching a yellow brontosaurus
balloon and watching the fat idea he loves
mingling in the sky with other noble ideas.
And think of his string that, even in this tossing wind, holds.

Grasshopper

When I come upon the grasshopper
on the porch, he lies nose down,
silent, looking not like a body
so much as some great damage,
like a car wreck. But I know
it wasn't an accident. Deciding
it needed to be done was the hard part.
He thought about it for a long time.
He loved his leg. But it was broken
and how could he grow another
until he got rid of the first?
One morning, he felt a tickle
he knew might be the new leg
trying to sprout. Carefully, he
pulled out of his long grief
and took the first bite.

The Scarf

It's still dark when I hear the heavy bong
    bong of the two-ton bell novitiates are ringing
        down the block at St. Charles Seminary

calling us, indifferent and lunatic, to prayer at six,
    and as I make coffee I do what it commands,
        release a prayer for you like a bird

into the morning sky, so dark, nothing's for certain,
    whether we'll end this day alive, whether our children
        will make it home again, and I remember

how it bonged its heart out last July at six,
    after the sky had been luminous for hours,
        the madness of summer light, what did the bell care

for that, or for the birds that wake so early, singing
    their monstrous hearts out? I make this bell
        stand for the only God I can imagine,

measuring the hours exactly, no matter what light says,
    so I'll have some measure to hold onto,
        to store up prayers against the bitter winter

that must be coming, grass growing wilder,
    light slamming her door like a bad mother, refusing to speak,
        squirrels mad with misplaced nuts, us cold in our coats,

and the cancer you fight more savage than the winter.
    You say you're better. The bell rings
        and rings. Last July, today, two ends of a scarf

we tie around our throats to keep the wind out.

—For Bill Leach

After the Tornado

Driving by Ridge and Swamp Pike this morning,
you can see prisoners
from the Montgomery County Jail
wading hip deep in grass,
picking up dentures, plastic dishes,
the little miracle of a hand mirror
that wasn't smashed.
And you can almost see
the newly dead blinking,
trying to get used to
their own roofs down there
no bigger than open matchbooks,
and the factory where, every morning,
they parked their cars,
now the size of a sow
with nursing piglets.

No wonder they stick around,
floating like wash,
looking down at maples
small as broccoli heads, until
it dawns on them
that anything so tiny
can go on without them,
and they ease away from
their human stories
long enough to practice

taking their eyes off the road,
which has become a gray snake
curving through the meadow.
When the cars keep driving
inside the white stitches,
they avert their eyes a while longer.
And when the lawns stay put,
you can almost hear their relief

that nothing will stop without them.
Like the wind vocalizing
its most trustworthy consonants,
they drift toward the curved margin
of the universe
where time forgets itself,
and turning for one last look,
they see the tiny thief,
released from his cell
for a whole morning,
handing the red purse
back to the housewife.

Insomnia

When I startle awake at 2 A.M.
    nothing seems wrong. The Arizona horizon
        goes on inside its steel frame,
drenched in a few hundred centuries

of yellow sunlight, while its cousin,
    the eggbeater, sleeps sweetly
        in its drawer, and Middle C,
godlike in its faithfulness,

goes on exerting two thousand pounds of pressure
    against the backboard of our piano.
        And yet my soul, shocked
from sleep by a nightmare,

worries and worries the same question.
    Meanwhile, my sweet, dumb body
        decides to go for a walk.
It is not pretty, this argument between them,

and it has gone on for fifty years.
    But out in the neighborhood,
        isn't it amazing
(the body thinks) how a simple nightshirt

can be woven of moonlight!
    How, under the wind-driven stars,
        the maples seem to be escaping.
The body loves everything,

even the terrified soul,
    which it calls and calls.
        The body has just begun to pad up the rise
by the Merion Tribute House

when it hears footsteps and then—for joy!—
    the soul falls in beside it, hands
        stuffed in her pockets, her slouchy *iamb,*
iamb trudging in the same direction toward sleep.

Luci's Knee

Your postcard: *Worse now, can't hike,*
tomorrow—surgery, and I can't help
but wonder where they'll put it
when the plastic one takes over. I think
of monstrous trucks tagged Medical
Waste, the way a lost limb still aches.
The way you love and long to keep
the knee you can't bend. Wishing I could

heal you, I'll do what I can. Stay where
you are. I'll make a cushion of this page,
Friend, and we will kneel to celebrate the knee
that's carried you to Jerusalem, oh rabbi
with its skullcap, knee that's tumbled
like a bumblebee among buddelia blossoms,
old elephant that recalls its ancient thrills
and injuries. Assume it was militant once

and wouldn't bend. I praise it. When it
was limber as water, I praise that, too.
I praise it entirely, kneeling here at the end,
until it takes off, your first installment,
bending before you do, in praise.
Oh hinge, oh bird in flight,
angel, messenger, knee, knee, knee,
speed, whinnying from this barn

into the far green grass of God's terrifying grace.

—*For Luci Shaw*

Geese, Tree, Apple, Leaves

Every angel is terrifying.
—Rainer Maria Rilke

Suppose you're blind, and so you can't see
the broken necklace of geese sailing the sky,

then tilt up your face and listen as their honking riles
the air. And if somehow you're going deaf as well,

the cries of geese receding on the wind,
then lay your hand on bark to feel the wind

that sways the apple tree. Or if you can't feel
the tree, then pick and eat one perfect apple,

or failing that, as rain gets out its knives
smell the fall, swift-falling in the leaves.

But oh, if all is growing dark, the darkness
swallowing up the tree, its apples, leaves, and geese,

and if you think a hawk is circling in the final
autumn air, then let the splendid angel

come, my friend, to read your rights to you,
quicksilver angel, angel of snow, the lover who

has waited all your life at your elbow.

—*For Carol Thomson*

Illinois Poetry Series

Laurence Lieberman, Editor

In the Black Window: New and
Selected Poems
Michael Van Walleghen (2004)

A Deed to the Light
Jeanne Murray Walker (2004)

National Poetry Series

Eroding Witness
Nathaniel Mackey (1985)
Selected by Michael S. Harper

The High Road to Taos
Martin Edmunds (1994)
Selected by Donald Hall

Palladium
Alice Fulton (1986)
Selected by Mark Strand

Theater of Animals
Samn Stockwell (1995)
Selected by Louise Glück

Cities in Motion
Sylvia Moss (1987)
Selected by Derek Walcott

The Broken World
Marcus Cafagña (1996)
Selected by Yusef Komunyakaa

The Hand of God and a Few
Bright Flowers
William Olsen (1988)
Selected by David Wagoner

Nine Skies
A. V. Christie (1997)
Selected by Sandra McPherson

The Great Bird of Love
Paul Zimmer (1989)
Selected by William Stafford

Lost Wax
Heather Ramsdell (1998)
Selected by James Tate

Stubborn
Roland Flint (1990)
Selected by Dave Smith

So Often the Pitcher Goes to Water
until It Breaks
Rigoberto González (1999)
Selected by Ai

The Surface
Laura Mullen (1991)
Selected by C. K. Williams

Renunciation
Corey Marks (2000)
Selected by Philip Levine

The Dig
Lynn Emanuel (1992)
Selected by Gerald Stern

Manderley
Rebecca Wolff (2001)
Selected by Robert Pinsky

My Alexandria
Mark Doty (1993)
Selected by Philip Levine

Theory of Devolution
David Groff (2002)
Selected by Mark Doty

Rhythm and Booze
Julie Kane (2003)
Selected by Maxine Kumin

Other Poetry Volumes

Local Men and *Domains*
James Whitehead (1987)

Her Soul beneath the Bone: Women's
Poetry on Breast Cancer
Edited by Leatrice Lifshitz (1988)

Days from a Dream Almanac
Dennis Tedlock (1990)

Working Classics: Poems on
Industrial Life
*Edited by Peter Oresick and Nicholas
Coles* (1990)

Hummers, Knucklers, and Slow
Curves: Contemporary Baseball
Poems
Edited by Don Johnson (1991)

The Double Reckoning of
Christopher Columbus
Barbara Helfgott Hyett (1992)

Selected Poems
Jean Garrigue (1992)

New and Selected Poems, 1962–92
Laurence Lieberman (1993)

The Dig and *Hotel Fiesta*
Lynn Emanuel (1994)

For a Living: The Poetry of Work
*Edited by Nicholas Coles and Peter
Oresick* (1995)

The Tracks We Leave: Poems on
Endangered Wildlife of North
America
Barbara Helfgott Hyett (1996)

Peasants Wake for Fellini's *Casanova*
and Other Poems
*Andrea Zanzotto; edited and translated
by John P. Welle and Ruth Feldman;
drawings by Federico Fellini and
Augusto Murer* (1997)

Moon in a Mason Jar and *What My
Father Believed*
Robert Wrigley (1997)

The Wild Card: Selected Poems, Early
and Late
*Karl Shapiro; edited by Stanley Kunitz
and David Ignatow* (1998)

Turtle, Swan and *Bethlehem in Broad
Daylight*
Mark Doty (2000)

Illinois Voices: An Anthology of
Twentieth-Century Poetry
*Edited by Kevin Stein and G. E.
Murray* (2001)

On a Wing of the Sun
Jim Barnes (3-volume reissue, 2001)

Poems
*William Carlos Williams; introduction
by Virginia M. Wright-Peterson* (2002)

Creole Echoes: The Francophone
Poetry of Nineteenth-Century
Louisiana
*Translated by Norman R. Shapiro;
introduction and notes by M. Lynn
Weiss* (2003)

Poetry from *Sojourner:* A Feminist
Anthology
*Edited by Ruth Lepson with Lynne
Yamaguchi; introduction by Mary
Loeffelholz* (2003)

Asian American Poetry: The Next
Generation
*Edited by Victoria M. Chang; foreword
by Marilyn Chin* (2004)

The University of Illinois Press
is a founding member of the
Association of American University Presses.

———————————————————

Composed in 10/13.5 Minion
with Minion display
by Celia Shapland
for the University of Illinois Press
Designed by Dennis Roberts
Manufactured by Sheridan Books, Inc.

University of Illinois Press
1325 South Oak Street
Champaign, IL 61820-6903
www.press.uillinois.edu